Run Your Business in Ten Essentials for 365 Days and Beyond!

A special on-the-go guide to turn to for business owners because you are the business. Oh YES!

Kala Jordan-Lindsey

Prologue

"You are the business, so never give up and go out of business. Just have faith you can do it and you will make it. Oh YES, you can! Never stop knowing it. Never stop saying it. Never stop showing it. Share it and wear it. Oh "YES" You are Ever Special!" -Kala

My neighbor said, "Yes, Karen and I grew up in this neighborhood for over twenty five years, and walked to Healthy Eats corner store wash house to sit, read, and socialize with others, as long as you and your wife were born. Lol! But after the first year, the owner's assistant fell ill, so he closed the wash house for a few months until his assistant recovered, which he generously provided her with sick pay, continued medical benefits, and blessed her with the opportunity to return to work, once she was back in good health. He never worried about losing business, because "he" represented the business. He ran his business in gratitude, love, passion, confidence, determination, zeal, humility, faith, compassion, and patience, therefore, he attracted everyone in the neighborhood, including children, and tourist all over the world. David, the owner said, "Now, Lindsey make sure you *Run Your Business in Ten Essentials for 365 Days and Beyond*" before you start your inspirational speaking business. Why, David? Because you'll never have to fear missing items. And simply because you "will" have days that will test your strength, mindset, faith, heart, purpose, and calling, so please follow my words of wisdom and advice. This keepsake is an effective, special, and on-the-go guidebook to inspire first-time business owners, entrepreneurs that are already running businesses, and for those who are simply thinking about starting their own business, to maintain a purposeful, meaningful, and impactful business during and beyond business hours for pleasing results!

If you're a first-time business owner, college students aspiring to become business owners, or already running your business with experience, the benefits of running your business with 150% gratitude, love, passion, confidence, determination, zeal, humility, faith, compassion, and patience will allow you to create, build, and grow into an effective, purposeful, meaningful,and impactful business with lasting results!

As a business owner, you're sometimes influenced with a thousand opinions, ideas, plans, quotes, and influencers, except your own. Red flag! If so, where's "your" business, thoughts, and ideas? It's not your pen and pad, emailing list, PowerPoint slides, best-selling products, computer, marketing team, video recordings, assistants, and swipe-card machine, but turn on your "light" and look in the mirror, it's "you," because oh YES! So, since "you" are responsible for running your business, Kala motivates and encourages you to build your business by activating these ten essentials, which will open your eyes to the "real business" in you! So, make special note that whether you're a business owner and run a fashion, hair, marketing, publishing, speaking, educational, consultant, food, financial corporation, music, writing, broadcast, podcast, administrative, health, tax, T-shirt, blogging, car wash, or lawn service business, know that in order to "stay in business" you must "be in business," letting this amazing and existing power run your business in ten essentials to maintain a purposeful, meaningful, and impactful business with lasting results.Oh YES!

BUSINESS ESSENTIAL #1

GRATITUDE

Run your business in the power of GRATITUDE!

You all are making me sweat as if I were on a treadmill bursting every story from my soul like the viewing of a child popping balloon after balloon after balloon! But, before I start and leave you on purpose, I'm sure you once heard someone say, "They fired the wrong person, but this time around I, "Lisa"stand as a surviving and grateful victim saying, Oh YES to all who have walked in my shoes! They fired the right person, at the right time, simply on purpose, so as a result of the unexpected, it fired me up with so much fuel of motivation, determination, hope, faith, love, compassion, forgiveness, zeal, and inspiration to open my eyes to the reality of not only my life, but life, on purpose as a business owner! I am no longer fearful, but fearless with a life-calling to unclog the trials and tribulations, struggles, mountains, battles, tradegies, and stories within my soul to inspire the world on purpose. Wow! What an outstanding and amazing speech, Lisa! You really touched my heart, and inspired me to love unconditionally, forgive, and to never give up when it seems impossible, despite coping with drugs and alcohol, mental and sexual abuse, and depression, after fifteen years. I lost my job in 2017, while dealing with health issues, financial problems, and depression, but after hearing your uplifting, funny, amazing, and inspirational story, you opened my eyes with tears, full on the reality of how special and blessed I am, as a beautiful, strong, and loving woman, wife, and mother, despite my struggles. Thank you so much, Lisa!" You're welcome, but more importantly, thank you for your kind and touching words! Oh YES!

Business owners, thank you, gracias, merci, grazie, danke Sehr sir, and madam "sounds" polite, but more so, when it rolls off the tip of your tongue and you simply say, "Thank you." This generous and special word should automatically sound from your heart, exiting your mouth, after any positive words, feedback, or comments are given to you or even if someone walks up to you and hands you a million dollars. Lol. Right? It may not exit automatically, but I encourage you to strive, with effort, to work on it, and just let it flow from your sound box, with purpose, to every person you encounter, during and beyond your business hours, for 365 Days and beyond.

As an observer, we sometimes take words of kindness and blessings we receive for granted, with the mindset that we're "supposed" to be thanked rather of "deserving." We don't, but it happens because we're blessed and amazingly special for our gifts and abilities to encourage, inspire, uplift, and motivate others.We hear "Thank you" in restaurants, shopping centers, educational institutions, at awards assemblies and banquets, meetings, in church congregations, and more, throughout the world, but mostly spoken on a condition. As business owners, I encourage you to cherish and take on the road for 365 Days and beyond, in your briefcases, but hearts, every word of kindness and generosity given to you. Thank you!

As business owners, when was the last time you said, "Thank you" to your customers, clients, staff, and an audience? Was it triggered on a condition or unconditionally? And red light, saying, "Thank you" has no identity and neither is it associated with race, ethnicity, gender, and age.Now, can you think back to when your mother gave you a special treat after completing a task or having made A's and B's on your report card? After she gave you the candy or ten dollars, you immediately said, "Thank you, mom!" Right? Well, just as you said, "Thank you" when you were young should continue now that you are an adult and wiser, so never stop knowing it. Never stop saying it. Never stop showing it. Share it and wear it- Thank you! It doesn't matter the language you speak and your nationality, "Thank you" flows in the veins of every human-being on this planet, which means there aren't any excuses. Just humble your heart, which will allow you to "activate" from your heart, off the tip of your tongue, the generous word, "Thank you" for 365 Days and beyond.

It's easier to stand in the position to be thanked, but to this day, it's still a challenge for many, especially when you're being served, to simply activate the word, "Thank you." There's just something really special, powerful, and engaging about this nine-letter word, "gratitude." It represents satisfactory and fulfilment like the last time, ladies, when you visited the emergency room with pregnancy contractions, you were given medicines and/or other solutions to help ease and relieve you sudden and gradual contractions after nothing worked at home-You were satisfied after remedies were given to you to help this natural sensation, which fulfilled and eased your issue, so you said, "Thank you" to the nurses.

I find it even more special, when you simply, say, "Thank you, effortlessly!" It should flow, like a beach ball floating across the ocean, through every vein and muscle in your body and roll off your tongue just as easy as the numbers, "one, two, three," as Michael Jackson once sang, but for some, it takes the process of learning, practicing, and just activating, which as business owners should be bring your joy, happiness, and keep you motivated, encouraged, uplifted, empowered, and inspired! Why? Because everday you're blessed, no matter who, what, when, where, why, and how, you are still breathing! As business owners, your business, represents every part of you like your personality, attitude, style, and brand so, without it, remember, you'd always be leaving something behind, clogged in your heart, and in your briefcase.

Based on experience, your business becomes more purposeful, meaningful, and impactful to the point where you are now "in love" with a strong connection and bond in your craft, gift, purpose, which positions you in your calling, when you master an attitude of gratitude, which realistically takes less than five seconds to speak.

So, the big question is how do you know that you've mastered gratitude? When you wake up saying, "Thank you," live, breath, walk, show, and speak gratitude, despite your situation, day, the number of sells, website traffic, Facebook, Twitter, Instagram, Pinterest, and Linkedin likes, and membership sign-ups for your business. You must grow in gratitiude and not with it. Why? Because when you live "in" gratitude, you have nothing to carry. It's tends to flow, effortlessy and automatically, but when you live "with" gratitude, you'd always be carrying an "extra" load in your briefcase. Just think about it, without thinking twice, that every "Thank you" equals opportunity to enhance and grow your business and brand to the next level. Your company will take off , impact, and inspire the world, so if you're going to take off, take off in gratitude and just say, "Thank you" for 365 Days and beyond, which produces a purposeful, meaningful, and impactful business as a result of activating a simple yet powerful word that can significantly affect the very success of your business now, today, and in the long run! Oh YES!

LIST YOUR SPECIAL REMINDERS

✓ _____

✓ _____

✓ _____

✓ _____

BUSINESS ESSENTIAL #2

LOVE

Run your business in the power of LOVE!

Hi dear, "I love you" is what we're expectedly and used to hearing, but how often do "you," as business owners not only say, "I love you," but walk out your doors and prove it through your actions? Is it ony when an exchange of goods and services are made or in the case, if you "feel" like it?" Are your clients, audience members, and staff loved, or are you just pretending or "acting out" love with a quick handshake and bye? Run "in" love instead of with love-Your business (you) will never run out of love if you run your business "in" love for 365 Days and beyond!

So, one of your supporting clients approaches you and says, "David, you conducted a magnificent educational conference on Monday. Man, I love you for all your support, patience, and compassion you gave every educator in the audience in the love your showed by treating everyone with your newest and best-selling book, "My Calling As An Educator," training course, and care package for an entire year! Wow! Who does that? The answer is love. So, since you understand the importance and power of "showing" love, you also said, "I love you too, John, thank you!" Love alert! Love understands, is humble, a peacemaker, caring, forgiving, supportive, self-less, compassionate, and does not boast, even as a business owner, during and beyond business hours.

Whether you're business owners or not, "love" does not and should not change the situation, envioronment, and circumstance, but should remain activated for 365 days and beyond because purpose, meaning, and impact flows from your heart! I motivate you to carry the mindset that your clients, employees, and "audience members" (every person you encounter and plus) "expect" you to care and love them, because face it, not only are they servicing you, you're also servicing them with something of great need, value, and benefit!

Do you remember the last time you traveled to a meeting, conference, workshop, brunch, or just a meeting with clients, and said, "Michelle, Carol, Jefferson, Justin, Evetta, and Karen, as the list goes on, I appreciate and thank you all for your consistent support. I love you?" If not, what did you say? The "power" of running your business in love is that you don't have to "go and get it," because thank you and love runs in your blood, through your heart, and executed with your actions.

On the other hand, how are you? "I'm grateful and loving every moment of growing in business, or did you complain and say, Oh, man, I'm down in sales and I'm not doing so good? Your business will run in purpose, meaning, and make an impact, once you learn, practice, and activate love! In other words, for your business to successfully function and prosper with blessings beyond your imagination, you must own, walk, and live in love, not with love.

On the other hand, as a business owner, you will be face and go against many ups and downs, client discrepancies, and loses, so instead of carrying love, live in love for 365 Days and beyond, for best results. If you don't appreciate and activate love, compassion, and humility which are already stored in your heart, as a business owner, it will impact your business. So, without love in your briefcase, your business will wither like the disappearance of smoke. Love is essential because it carries 100% of the power that will take your business to the next level, deal with clients, and grow in purpose, meaning, and impact lives. Oh YES!

LIST YOUR SPECIAL REMINDERS

- ✓ _____
- ✓ _____
- ✓ _____
- ✓ _____

BUSINESS ESSENTIAL #3

PASSION

Run your business in the power of PASSION!

Cynthia states, "If it weren't for having experienced an unexpected employment battle two years ago, my eyes would not have opened to the point where I am conscious of my purpose and life calling.Therefore, because I'm living in my purpose, which gives me unexplainable, yet explainable passion, I'm grateful and in love with this amazing and pleasing crave to express myself through writing. So, in other words, in my struggles, created my passion, and at that point, revealed my life calling as a grateful survivor, author and business owner, inspiring the world through my visible voice! And because I run my business in the power of passion, I'll never forget to execute a hundred and fifty percent in all that I do and give for 365 Days and beyond.

So, you're probably still wondering, well, what is she saying? Well, Cynthia's struggles not only prepared her, but positioned her in an amazing place in her life to finally fulfil a passion she always dreamt of, which is activating her life calling as an author! Cynthia says, "I've never experienced writing with so much zeal, gratitude, appreciation, and passion until my battles. Every word represents such an amazing expression that I love writing as if I were making love, with so much expression, purpose, meaning, and impact!

Cecil, New York's top event planner approaches and her and says, "Hi, Cynthia! Because of your amazing attitude, zeal, strength, and inspirational story, as a published author and speaker for over ten years, I'd like to invite you out to speak in front of a group of ten women at a local drug rehab for an hour.We only have a budget of $750.00. Is this acceptable? Oh yes! Okay. Wonderful, and can we count on you? Yes, of course, you can, Cecil! Thank you! Cynthia's story and passion motivated, uplifted, and inspired her to say, "Yes!" What would you have said?

Purpose has neither a title and label, but rather, means your simply "living" and doing exactly what's suppose to occur today, now, at this hour, in your life.But, on the other hand, passion executes when you just "let" it happen. So, if you are running your business in your purpose, which is also a gift, as a finanicial consultant, let your passion just "speak", without force and effort. In other words, show and prove it, rather than tell. You prove your passion without identification, but internally and naturally from your heart, by putting your heart and soul in everything you say and do, with a hundred and fifty percent gratitude, love, joy, zeal, and drive for 365 Days and beyond. Passion also has no identity and physicality, but is "alive" and "activated" when you step out in order to be outstanding to inspire and help make a difference in your business, which creates impact!

As business owners, don't deactivate your passion; which once again, is ia gift.In other words, don't just let your passion "sit and hide" over the motive of profit just because it makes you happy, but rather, because your passionate in your purpose! Your passion is executed and more profitable when you activate an attitude of gratitude, originality, humility, appreciation, and thirst to express and show the special person you were born and blessed to be! So, ladies and gentleman, run your business in the power of passion 24-hours a day, seven days a week, and for 365 Days and beyond. I motivate you not to wait until your "doors" open or you "step into your business wear" to say, "Thank you," and to inspire with passion, a smile, laugh, dance, and motivate.So, express your love of life in your purpose with 150% passion!

So, are you the business owner who naturally draws others towards you, with your pleasant and humble personality and attitude, "voice," love, compassion, respect, zeal, dedication, and passion or do you draw customers away because you're pleasant and humble, but your passion is "limited" just for the sell? There's no way possible to run your business in passion with imitation, since "you" are the passion. It's like saying, " I am limited in giving passion in my writing, but unlimited when I'm on stage." o even if you were without pen

Passion circulates through your blood 24-hours a day, seven days a week, for 365 Days and beyond, just activate it! Remember, there are no limits neither boundaries in passion because it can be executed at all times, no matter who, what, when, where, why, and how. Passion represents the "voice" of your business, which is "yourself." Without it, no one "hears" you and you become invisible to the world, no matter how much time, effort, money you spend, and influences in your circle, passion exposes itself, through time. In other words, passion speaks louder than words, is deeper than the lake in your backyard and brand joined together, never sleeps, but alive 24-hours, just activate it. You are blessed to be business owners because you're living in your purpose, therefore, be on fire to inspire, motivate, love, develop relationships, listen, encourage, empower, and make an impact simply because your business is meaningful (special). Remember, in order to appreciate, value, give 150%, engage your audience and clients through your passion."Natural" passion expresses and executes any day and anytime. Live, walk, and breath in your passion, which is found in your purpose! If your passion is on "mute," just continue living with a positive, humble, appreciative, and grateful heart, and it will sound! Oh YES!

LIST YOUR SPECIAL REMINDERS

✓ _____

✓ _____

✓ _____

✓ _____

BUSINESS ESSENTIAL #4

CONFIDENCE

Run your business in the power of CONFIDENCE!

As you sit back and reflect on the growth of your business for a year, you realize there hasn't been much website traffic, product sales, subscribers, and engagements, despite all the hard work, monthly and yearly business fees, energy, enthusiasm, videos, and late night recordings, but you're still in business! You're still in business because you own and running your business in gratitude, passion, and have a deep appreciation and love in your purpose with confidence! You understand that everything apart of your business doesn't identify the business, but if you're still standing, you'll always "remain" in business simply because "you" are the real business and your faith and hope leaves you with nothing less than confidence!

Yesterday, you walked up to the podium of your first business conference and said, "After experiencing an unexpected employment battle, I didn't remain seated, but instead, I was inspired to activate my other gifts by starting my own speaking business, which had allowed me to write and soon publish, books within my soul. So, April 2018, I started my business and now it has been alittle over a year that my business has been open, but now I've come to finally realize, I don't have the best marketing team, but I'm still confident. I don't have much website traffic, but I'm still confident. I don't have a huge staff, but I'm still condident. And, I don't have the best PowerPoint slides, booked events, a lot of products, and a six-figure salary, but guess what? I'm still confident! No matter who, what, when, where, why, and how, remember, with confidence as business owners, you can make, you can do it, oh yes, you can! You have the potential and can achieve it, with the right mindset, focus, determination, hope, faith, and confidence.

Confidence maintains a lasting, purposeful, meaning and impactful business, despite the ups and downs you will face, income fluctuations, and business traffic. Without confidence for

365 days and beyond, your business will remain just "another" business verses "the" business that stands out as outstanding so, just "be" the business your were born and blessed to be.Oh YES!

LIST YOUR SPECIAL REMINDERS

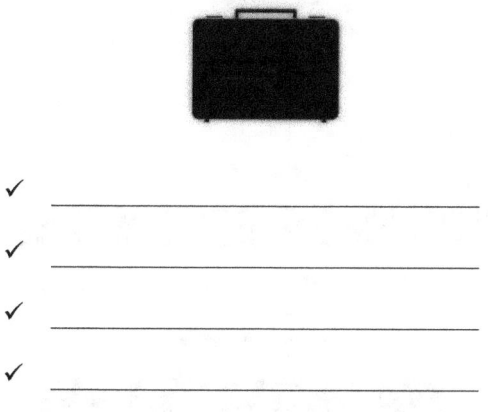

✓ _____

✓ _____

✓ _____

✓ _____

BUSINESS ESSENTIAL #5

COMPASSION

Run your business in the power of COMPASSION!

So, the CEO of the National Health Department (Denzel) sends you a special invitation that reads, "The department and I would be honored to have you, Gabriala Grisby, present an hour workshop and speak about your new pharmaceutical business for all non-insured patients around the world, next month. We have a buduget of $17,000.00, but also informed your newest book "The Nurse Boss," was recently released, therefore we'd be enthused to also purchase five hundred copies of your book, but we'd be unable to provide you compensation for hotel accommodation and airfare for two days in Houston, Texas, but since we know you have to eat, Gabriala, we'd go ahead and provide you with a gift card for meals too. How does that sound? It would be an priveledge and true blessing. So, do you accept this offer?" Oh yes, of course, Denzel! Please send me the contract and I'd be happy to return them to you! I'm enthused and can't wait! You were blessed and so you said, "yes!" because you not only ran your business with gratitude, passion, zeal, and humility, but also with 150% compassion. Gabriala can remember, before obtaining her nursing license, buying a home, and car, that she was homeless for five years and hit "rock bottom" with just the clothes on her back and a bed mat, eating out of garbage cans, without medical insurance. Her story of trials and tribulations, battles, and having experienced a financial valley, led her to say, "yes," even more, now that she's a a grateful, strong, and successful survivor, her story opened her eyes to have such a heart full of compassion, now earning six-figures, as a business owner and author.

Always carry compassion, first in your heart, briefcase, during and beyond your business hours. It doesn't matter the color, size, and how organize your business plan is written out, you will loose blessings. With little or no compassion, your business will just remain as a window display where the world just "stops by," but doesn't want your service because you, the business owner is not determined to show up and show out to be outstanding with compassion.

LIST YOUR SPECIAL REMINDERS

✓ _____

✓ _____

✓ _____

✓ _____

BUSINESS ESSENTIAL #6

ZEAL

Run your business in the power of ZEAL!

Wow! Look at this woman, wife, and mother on stage. Despite her story, she shows so much zeal. It's breathtaking! And look at me, she's not sweating and looking into our eyes because their absolutely beautiful.Well, of course they are, but it's deeper than just our eyes. I'm telling you, but more so, listen to me- This woman has a profound and unique story that intentionally lights up the stage and the entire world with her amazing and visible voice. Every sweat and tear represents the struggles, battles, tragedies, and success she's experienced. I read about her story last week with my girls, and Jeff, she's absolutely amazing, motivational, touching, sweet, and a strong and grateful survivor with so much passion and zeal that will inspire you on purpose! I've been a client of hers for years, and when I listen to her testimonies, and stories within her soul, she transformed my mindset about life, encouraged, uplifted, and inspired me on fire for 365 days and on. After losing my job of twelve years of study, I became ill, lose weight, depressed, and my family and I hit rock bottom. When it happened, it was unexpected. I didn't know what to do or even say. I thought my heart was going to pop out of my chest, but thank God, it didn't. I prayed and prayed and eventually came across Imani's webpage. I read through it, watched her videos and blogs, and was immediately touched and inspired to purchase her books, Cds, and invited her to speak to the young ladies at the Young Women Voices organization, which Jeff, she knocked the socks off every woman's feet with an outstanding, powerful, engaging, and inspirational story with so much passion that also left every single audience member speechless to speaking their visible voices while knowing how beautiful and special they are!

"Never stop knowing it. Never stop saying it. Never stop showing it. Share it and wear it. Oh YES!" Where's your zeal? Is it just on stage or is it also activated when you're writing, selling products, attending meetings, traveling, coaching, motivating and inspiring others, and on the phone? Just as man loves unconditionally, unconditional zeal as a business owner will keep you in business. Unconditional zeal will also keep you motivated, driven, and inspired for 365 Days and beyond. Zeal immediately tells your audience and clients about your personality and attitude, and will even affect whether or not they want your service.So, if your heart is still beating and you're alive, remain thankful and run your business in zea! And remember, zeal allows you to prosper, grow, gain, and maintain an unstoppable mindset of determination, hope, and faith, like no other. Just simply live in zeal because you have an amazing gift, purpose, meaning, impact, and visible voice! Oh YES!

LIST YOUR SPECIAL REMINDERS

✓ _____

✓ _____

✓ _____

✓ _____

BUSINESS ESSENTIAL #7

HUMILITY

Run your business in the power of HUMILITY!

Hi, Robert! Did you hear about the forty- thousand dollar grant I was just awarded for, for my nonprofit children's T-shirt organization in Miami? I am so proud of myself for doing all the work, phone calls, meetings, grant proposels, and so now I'm enjoying boasting about all this money I have to all my friends and family. I've even made thousand announcements on every social media page, radio stations, and educational institutions, that yes, I did it, yes, yes, I did it! . And wait, oh yes, I also called up your buddy and bragged about how much more money I received than he did. I also heard the big announcement that you received a big grant as well.Did you? Yes, I sure did! Did you also boast? No, Robert, I didn't. Listen, running your business with a "boastful or prideful" attitude is not the mindset to carry and show, but with a humble and grateful attitude, you will always succeed, gain, grow, and provide a greater impact to your community, clients, audience, and staff, so although it's exciting, just smile and remain on fire with gratitude and zeal! Thank you, Joseph, for your words of wisdom , advice, and encouragement. You're right. The moment I started to boast, I felt as if I were behind a dark window, with so much pressure, like a heavy load of clothes being thrown against my brain, unexpectedly. You're awesome and I truly love you for sharing your kindness!

When you run your business "with" humility verses "in" humility, you may have a tendency to "forget" to be humble, because you're being forced to carry an "extra" load for results not activivated "in" your heart.But, instead, when you choose to run your business "in: humility, you will always win and live with an unexplainable attitude of appreciation, gratitude, and love that will take your business (you) to the next level! Since you're running your business "in" humility, you're worry-free of carrying anything. It's like watching a gifted comedian on stage-Because Kevin Hart is naturally funny, he doesn't have to force himself to be funny, because it's a natural gift. He doesn't have to "carry" jokes, they're executed from within. Before he walks out on stage, he's "filled" and "ready." As a result in running your business in humility, you will also reap successful business growth and mind-blowing opportunities!

So, imagine you've been the CEO of Oh YES Fashion N'spire Design for fifteen years and yesterday your best friend, who's a first-time business owner, also in fashion, was asked to present a national workshop at this year's fashion convention in Europe, so when she informed you about it, you smiled, congratulated her and said, "Congratulations! You definitely deserve it!" Humility was shown the moment you congratulated her and said she deserved it, despite how many years of experience and education you have. So, now that you finally undstand and have applied the ten essentials to running your business, your attitude has transformed from living selfish to selfless, over a period of time.And just some words of wisdom- Never leave your front door without showing, but "owning" humility!

Humility let's go and lets others receive the honor, instead of the developing envy and jealously. As business owners, competition will always exist, but with understanding that life happens on purpose, for a reason, and in realizing everyone has a season, it will allow you to rise above and overcome the fear of your competitiors! Be fearless because you are humble! In fact, knowing there's competition in your neighborhood, city, state, and in the world should actually force you to live in humility. In otherwords, just "wait your turn and your number will be called!"

Possessing a humble attitude will also allow you to inspire, motivate, and empower others to activate the same. So, remember to never leave humility apart from you, but live "in" humility for 365 Days and beyond because there's purpose, your business has unexplainable meaning, and executes with guaranteed impact. Oh YES!

LIST YOUR SPECIAL REMINDERS

✓ _____

✓ _____

✓ _____

✓ _____

BUSINESS ESSENTIAL #8

DETERMINATION

Run your business in the power of DETERMINATION!

Evetta and Pete Grisby are not only business owners, but siblings. They own a cleaning company they just initiated and are very enthused with joy about planning their launch party in a week, so in the midst of making preparations, their cars and $20,000 business loan gets stolen, blocks away from their home. And their launch party is three days away. Yikes! So, in the back of your mind, what are you thinking? Well, of course I know what you're thinking, but why not stop and step on the path of running your business in determination? Evetta and Pete had faith, hope, and were very determined that they'd recoup their loss before their grand opening. So, they prayed and immediately reached out to the police, who successfully recouped their belongings without one penny missing, just in time for Evetta and Pete's big day!

Why isn't your business going anywhere? You're in the same location as last year. Closed and out of business. Could it be that you have no determination? Your desk, hard work, skills, gifts, emails, and "Open" sign are in the same spot and chamber as a year ago with nothing except blessings before you. I dare you to open your eyes and put on your vision glasses, but wait, can you drive or are you afraid because you're not focused, strength, and no energy?

Without determination, a unique formula of faith, passion plus zeal, and confidence, your business and hard work in your calling goes nowhere, except clogged and useless. Every customer that approaches you only "window shops" because the business (you) has no determination. So, in order to "drive," you must step out and into the car, just the mindset of driving with determination-You must step out in order to step in determination. In other words, you can't execute unless you run your business "in" determination. You must be "prepared and ready" at all times to drive with confidence and zeal like no other! So, when you mark, get set, go and run your business in determination because your purpose is to help, empower, and inspire others through your gift, craft, but amazing calling, which has unexplainable meaning, and impact! You must be determined to drive in order to get gain untouchable confidence and self-esteem and to get you where you're suppose to be going. So, never forget the keys to running your business in determination, which is your heart. You will always need it to get anywhere in life and to run your business for 365 Days and beyond with purpose, meaning, and impact! Drive with determination because oh YES!

LIST YOUR SPECIAL REMINDERS

✓ _____

✓ _____

✓ _____

✓ _____

BUSINESS ESSENTIAL #9

FAITH

Run your business in the power of FAITH!

You sold over a hundred thousand copies of your first book and earned your first million dollars. Yes, wow, wow, wow! I've always wondered the same but realized it's simply because of one's level of "outstanding faith." Velma earned her first million dollars, ever, because her faith was "activated" the entire two years she walked through the process of publishing her first book and starting her business. Wow! Imagine having this type of faith for 365 Days and beyond. As an author and business owner of your own publishing company, would you have ever imagined or exercised "outstanding faith" if you really knew you'd profit your first million dollars, with daily and consistent effort, hope, motivation, zeal, focus, determination, and faith?

"Outstanding faith" takes more than just your faith, but faith beyond your understanding. Outstandig faith is strong, determined, and unstoppable, everyday, month, year, and in all circumstances and situations. I challenge you as business owners to go for it, with faith like you know that you know that you know, that oh yes, you can do it, you will make it, oh yes, you can! With "outstanding faith" your business will grow, succeed, and remain open because purpose, meaning, and impact drives your motive! So, never give up in your calling of running your business "in" faith!

I challenge you to activate "faith," believing that oh yes, your business goals will happen, with the right motive, mindset, purpose, focus, and faith like no other! So, my question is, do you really have faith in order to get from point A to point C? You must have faith, but not just from point A to C, but from point A to B as well. It's the small steps and risk one takes that help strengthen and develop unstoppable and "outstanding faith," especially when you're in the driver's seat as a business owner and behind the scenes, "going for it" with the unbelievable strength and faith. Remember, because your purpose as a hair stylist is to please and satisfy your customers, running your business "in" faith that all your hard work, practice, and workshops you will and has finally paid off, so "just do it" in faith! Oh YES!

LIST YOUR SPECIAL REMINDERS

✓ _____

✓ _____

✓ _____

✓ _____

BUSINESS ESSENTIAL #10

PATIENCE

Run your business in the power of PATIENCE!

Are you a business owner that can't seem to show patience because you're so busy and want your business to run perfectly? Did you overlook a client or phone call because you were too busy? Did you miss a sell because you were too busy to provide details or free shipping? Patience is essential and must be activated before you simply run anywhere and anything in life, like your business. So, because you are the business, it's okay for things not to run perfectly because you're not perfect. I motivate you to just run "in" patience!

With said, it's the end of the year and your administrative assistant has not completed two weeks worth of work-Invoice reports, incoming/outgoing emails for the new year, scheduled phone calls, and has not informed you about a $80,000 speaking engagement offer in a week. So, you become highly upset and inpatient with hearing her story. So, you become very upset, refuse to communicate and meet with her, and have no compassion,immediately terminating her position. Jennifer spent ten years of hard work, commitment, and dedication with your company, but since you, as the business owner didn't activate love, compassion, the heart to sit down and listen to her story, and patience, you wrongfully terminated her position. She finally spoke to you and said, "I've been behind because I've been coping with medical issues and depression, so, after hearing her story with compassion, you apologized, and activated more patience, which transformed your total mindset about life and running your business. Without love, compassion, a positive attitude, willingness to "listen" to others, and patience, your business will not run, but remain as your customer's window shoppoing opportunity- Parked and isolated just for viewing.

Patience is one of the most challenging and hardest essentials because it requires a hundred and fifty percent action-Consistency and daily effort. Don't doubt yourself, but just go for it and "live," in which you'll then discover your purpose and calling, which will amaze you with so much meaning and produce outstanding impact! And remember, because your business has purpose, meaning, and impacts every part of your business (you) and the world, always run your business "in" patience, but also in every other essential, for 365 Days and beyond. So, just do it because oh YES!

LIST YOUR SPECIAL REMINDERS

✓ _____

✓ _____

✓ _____

✓ _____

Oh "YES" You Are Ever Special!

Inspirational Speaker
Kala Jordan-Lindsey
Kala@visiblevoiceohyes.com
www.visiblevoiceohyes.com

Image Credit: AJ Distique Photography

Kala Jordan-Lindsey was born on August 14, 1986 in Delray Beach, Florida. She's one of four sisters (Jennifer, Allison, Heather and Aimee) of parents, Jefferson and Evetta Jordan and has two step sisters, Kanetra and Tamiera. She's happily married to Anthony Lindsey and has two beautiful daughters, Kamaria and Tamia Lindsey, who are truly special and a blessing in their lives. Kala's experience includes more than ten years as an educator and clarinetist and has a BM in Music Performance from Florida Atlantic University in Boca Raton, Florida and MM in Music Performance from Florida International University in Miami, Florida. She has taught throughout Palm Beach, Broward, and Miami-Dade County and blessed with the privilege to lead as an adjunct professor and faculty clarinetist at Miami Dade College Kendall Campus. She also performed in professional orchestras and bands and received numerous awards, including Teacher of the Year with the Miami Music Project and traveled to New York City to teach and perform in the New York Summer Music Festival. There are amongst many who also inspires her such as her parents, husband and daughters, mother-in-law, sisters, aunts and uncles, cousins, nieces and nephews, and ministers/wives. Kala is also the owner of inspirational speaking business, Visible Voice Oh YES! which she initiated in April 2018, after experiencing a life-changing obstacle. Besides her background in music, as a clarinetist, her gift and passion in her life-calling for expressing herself through speaking and writing has led her to write multiple books in which will be published in the near future- "Opened Eyes," a non-fiction inspirational book, "Oh YES Amira and Dorian," a childrens book, "My Loud Voice," non-fiction inspirational blog, "The Oatmeal Factory," a fairytale, and "Music for Children Learner's," a music educational book!" She says, "I am truly humble and grateful for every moment I'm blessed to stand before an audience to inspire, encourage, motivate, and empower oridanry human-beings as myself!" Kala is the woman, wife, and mother on the mic that smiles and will leave your audience inspired, without a doubt, knowing how special they are! She says, "You are the business! Never stop knowing it. Never stop saying it. Never stop showing it. Share it and wear it. Oh "YES" You are Ever Special!"

Have you always desired to run a successful and profitable business or maybe you're running a successful business with all that you'd desired? For some, I'm sure you carried what you wanted like a pen and note pad, computer, client forms, email list, portable swipe-card machine, and of course all your best-selling books, courses, and other outstanding products. Why not? You worked hard, spent money, and teamed up with the best coaches around to achieve it, right? But, wait a minute, what did you really carry beyond "Your" business clock and closed doors? Did you carry what you wanted or the essentials, like gratitude, passion, love, faith, confidence, compassion, determination, humility, zeal, and patience? Did you work hard with the mindset to gain for yourself or did you help others, with a minimum execution of words of wisdom and encouragement to the hunger to inspire? Did you reach out to the first-time business owners who were struggling to start their business or college students desiring to start their own business? Carrying these ten essentials will bless you unimaginably with a purposeful, meaningful, and impactful business, even when times get tough and your profit is low, so don't focus on "likes," boasting, becoming number one, having a perfect slide show, and speaking perfectly with all the right words and sentences, but instead, remain humble, strong, and desire to give a hundred and fifty percent as you live to run your business in your calling as you "speak" your amazing and powerful story! As business owners, I challenge you to reflect on purpose, meaning, and the impact of your business, during and beyond your business hours. Whether you're the CEO and run a fashion, marketing, publishing, speaking, educational, consultant, food, financial corporation, music, writing, commercial, administrative, tax, T-shirt, blogging, or lawn business, without purpose in your business, you will lack giving a hundred and fifty percent of gratitude, love, passion, confidence, drive, zeal, humility, faith, compassion, and patience, so go for it because oh YES!

www.ingramcontent.com/pod-product-compliance
Lightning Source LLC
Chambersburg PA
CBHW081023170526
45158CB00010B/3141